# Singapore MATH

# MENTAL MATH

## Strategies and Process Skills to Develop Mental Calculation

## Grade 6
### (Level 5)

**Frank Schaffer**

An imprint of Carson-Dellosa Publishing LLC

Greensboro, North Carolina

# CREDITS

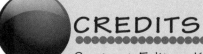

Content Editor: Karen Cermak-Serfass
Copy Editor: Barrie Hoople
Layout Design: Van Harris

This book has been correlated to state, common core state, national, and Canadian provincial standards. Visit www.carsondellosa.com to search for and view its correlations to your standards.

Copyright © 2011, Singapore Asian Publications (S) Pte Ltd

Frank Schaffer
An imprint of Carson-Dellosa Publishing LLC
PO Box 35665
Greensboro, NC 27425 USA

ISBN 978-1-936024-12-4
02-063131151

# ABOUT THIS BOOK

Welcome to Singapore Math! The national math curriculum used in Singapore has been recognized worldwide for its excellence in producing students highly skilled in mathematics. The country's students have ranked at the top in achievement in the world on the Trends in International Mathematics and Science Study (TIMSS) in 1993, 1995, 2003, and 2008. The study also shows that students in Singapore are typically one grade level ahead of students in the United States. Because of these trends, Singapore Math has gained interest and popularity.

Mathematics in the Singapore primary (elementary) curriculum covers fewer topics but in greater depth. Key math concepts are introduced and built upon to reinforce various mathematical ideas and thinking. Singapore Math curriculum aims to help students develop the necessary math process skills for everyday life and to provide students with the opportunity to master math concepts.

*Mental Math Level 5*, for grade 6, provides a comprehensive guide for mastering mental calculation. Each strategy in this book helps students perform mental calculation and obtain accurate answers in the shortest possible amount of time.

This book consists of 52 practice and review pages. Each practice page demonstrates a strategy with an example and includes 10 problems for students to solve. Students can then test their understanding by working on the review pages that are located after the practice pages.

To help students build and strengthen their mental calculation skills, this book provides strategies that will benefit students as they learn tips to solve math problems quickly and effectively. After acquiring such invaluable skills, students can apply them to their future, real-life experiences with math, such as in shopping and banking. *Mental Math Level 5* is an indispensable resource for all students who wish to master mental strategies and excel in them.

# TABLE OF CONTENTS

**Strategies Overview** ...................................................... **6**

WEEK 1 STRATEGY   Addition: Rounding Large Numbers Beginning with 9 ........... **8**

WEEK 2 STRATEGY   Addition: Breaking Up Numbers ................................................ **9**

WEEK 3 STRATEGY   Subtraction: Breaking Up Numbers .................................... **10**

WEEK 4 STRATEGY   Subtraction: Reverse Three-Digit Numbers ........................ **11**

WEEK 5   **General Review 1** .................................................... **12**

WEEK 6 STRATEGY   Rearranging to Multiply by 100 .................................... **13**

WEEK 7 STRATEGY   Rearranging to Multiply by 1,000 .................................. **14**

WEEK 8 STRATEGY   Double the 50 ...................................................... **15**

WEEK 9 STRATEGY   Multiplying Four-Digit Numbers by 11 .......................... **16**

WEEK 10   **General Review 2** .................................................... **17**

WEEK 11 STRATEGY   Multiplying Numbers by 12 ...................................... **18**

WEEK 12 STRATEGY   Multiplying Numbers by 15 ...................................... **19**

WEEK 13 STRATEGY   Multiplying Numbers by 25 ...................................... **20**

WEEK 14 STRATEGY   Multiplying Numbers by 50 ...................................... **21**

WEEK 15   **General Review 3** .................................................... **22**

WEEK 16 STRATEGY   Division: Breaking Up Divisors .................................. **23**

WEEK 17 STRATEGY   Division: Finding Remainders When Dividing by 5 ............... **24**

WEEK 18 STRATEGY   Division: Finding Remainders When Dividing by 8 ............... **25**

WEEK 19 STRATEGY   Division: Finding Remainders When Dividing by 9 ............... **26**

WEEK 20   **General Review 4** .................................................... **27**

WEEK 21 STRATEGY   Division: Dividing Numbers by 25 ................................ **28**

WEEK 22 STRATEGY   Adding Fractions with Unlike Denominators ........................ **29**

WEEK 23 STRATEGY   Subtracting Fractions with Unlike Denominators .................. **30**

WEEK 24 STRATEGY   Multiplying Fractions and Whole Numbers ........................ **31**

WEEK 25   **General Review 5** .................................................... **32**

WEEK 26 STRATEGY   Multiplying Identical Mixed Numbers with the Fraction $\frac{1}{2}$ ... **33**

WEEK 27 STRATEGY   Multiplying Mixed Numbers with Identical Fractions When the Numerator Is 1 ...................................................... **34**

WEEK 28 STRATEGY   Multiplying Mixed Numbers with Identical Whole Numbers .... **35**

WEEK 29 STRATEGY   Dividing Fractions by Whole Numbers ............................ **36**

# TABLE OF CONTENTS

| | | |
|---|---|---|
| WEEK 30 | **General Review 6** | 37 |
| WEEK 31 STRATEGY | Converting Fractions to Percentages | 38 |
| WEEK 32 STRATEGY | Percentage: 5% of a Number | 39 |
| WEEK 33 STRATEGY | Percentage: 15% of a Number | 40 |
| WEEK 34 STRATEGY | Percentage: 20% of a Number | 41 |
| WEEK 35 | **General Review 7** | 42 |
| WEEK 36 STRATEGY | Percentage: 45% of a Number | 43 |
| WEEK 37 STRATEGY | Squaring Numbers Ending with 5 | 44 |
| WEEK 38 STRATEGY | Squaring Numbers Beginning with 9 | 45 |
| WEEK 39 STRATEGY | Squaring Numbers Ending with 7 | 46 |
| WEEK 40 | **General Review 8** | 47 |
| WEEK 41 STRATEGY | Squaring Numbers Ending with 8 | 48 |
| WEEK 42 STRATEGY | Squaring Numbers Ending with 9 | 49 |
| WEEK 43 STRATEGY | Squaring Numbers from 40 to 50 | 50 |
| WEEK 44 STRATEGY | Adding a Series of Consecutive Numbers | 51 |
| WEEK 45 STRATEGY | Adding a Series of Numbers | 52 |
| WEEK 46 | **General Review 9** | 53 |
| WEEK 47 | **General Review 10** | 54 |
| WEEK 48 | **General Review 11** | 55 |
| WEEK 49 | **General Review 12** | 56 |
| WEEK 50 | **General Review 13** | 57 |
| WEEK 51 | **General Review 14** | 58 |
| WEEK 52 | **General Review 15** | 59 |
| ANSWER KEY | | 61 |

*The following overview provides examples of the various math problem types and skill sets taught in Singapore Math.*

**1 Addition: Rounding Large Numbers Beginning with 9**

999,900 + 999,800

999,900 ≈ 1,000,000     Step 1: Round each number up to the
(999,900 + 100)             nearest million.
999,800 ≈ 1,000,000
(999,800 + 200)

999,900 + 999,800      Step 2: Add the millions. Subtract the
= (1,000,000 + 1,000,000) − 200 − 100   amount needed to round up in
= (2,000,000 − 200) − 100     Step 1 from the sum.
= 1,999,800 − 100       Step 3: Subtract to find the answer.
= **1,999,700**

**2 Addition: Breaking Up Numbers**

699,000 + 101,000
= (690,000 + 100,000) + (9,000 + 1,000)  ❑ Break up the numbers for
= 790,000 + 10,000         easy addition.
= **800,000**

**3 Subtraction: Breaking Up Numbers**

199,980 − 99,800
= (199,800 + 180) − 99,800  ❑ Break up the first number for
= 199,800 − 99,800 + 180     easy subtraction.
= 100,000 + 180         ❑ Subtract the larger numbers.
= **100,180**              Add the remaining number
                   to the difference to find the
                   answer.

**4 Subtraction: Reverse Three-Digit Numbers**

895 − 598

8 − 5 = 3          Step 1: Find the difference of the
                hundreds digits in both numbers.
3 × 100 = 300      Step 2: Multiply the difference obtained
                in Step 1 by 100.
300 − 3 = 297      Step 3: Subtract the difference obtained
895 − 598 = **297**    in Step 1 from the product obtained
                in Step 2.

**6 Rearranging to Multiply by 100**

25 × 89 × 4
25 × 89 × 4 = 89 × 25 × 4  ❑ Arrange the numbers to create
                the factor 100.
= 89 × 100        ❑ Multiply the remaining factor by
= **8,900**          100 to find the answer.

**7 Rearranging to Multiply by 1,000**

125 × 860 × 8
125 × 860 × 8 = 860 × 125 × 8  ❑ Arrange the numbers to create
                the factor 1,000.
= 860 × 1,000      ❑ Multiply the remaining factor by
= **860,000**       1,000 to find the answer.

**8 Double the 50**

68 × 50
68 × 50 = 68 × 100 ÷ 2  ❑ Replace the factor 50 with 100 ÷ 2.
= 68 ÷ 2 × 100      ❑ Arrange the equation. Divide the first
= 34 × 100         factor by 2. Multiply the quotient by 100
= **3,400**          to find the answer.

**9 Multiplying Four-Digit Numbers by 11**

5,243 × 11
Step 1: The first and last digits of the number will be the first and last
        digits of the answer.
        First digit of the answer: **5**
        Last digit of the answer: **3**
Step 2: To find the middle three digits, start with the left and add
        each digit to the digit next to it.

| first digit | | | | last digit |
|---|---|---|---|---|
| 5 | (5 + 2) | (2 + 4) | (4 + 3) | 3 |
| 5 | 7 | 6 | 7 | 3 |

5,243 × 11 = **57,673**

**11 Multiplying Numbers by 12**

58 × 12
58 × 12 = (50 × 12) + (8 × 12)  ❑ Expand the first factor. Multiply both
                parts by 12.
= 600 + 96         ❑ Add the products to find the answer.
= **696**

**12 Multiplying Numbers by 15**

78 × 15
78 × 15 = (78 × 10) + (78 × 5)  ❑ Expand 15 into 10 and 5. Multiply the
                first factor by both 10 and 5.
= 780 + 390       ❑ Add the products to find the answer.
= **1,170**

**13 Multiplying Numbers by 25**

63 × 25
63 × (25 × 4)       ❑ Multiply 25 by 4 to make 100.
= (63 × 100) ÷ 4    ❑ Find the product and divide by 4
= 6,300 ÷ 4       to find the answer.
= **1,575**

**14 Multiplying Numbers by 50**

57 × 50
57 × (50 × 2)       ❑ Multiply 50 by 2 to make 100.
= (57 × 100) ÷ 2    ❑ Find the product and divide by 2
= 5,700 ÷ 2       to find the answer.
= **2,850**

**16 Division: Breaking Up Divisors**

2,880 ÷ 24
2,880 ÷ 24 = 2,880 ÷ (4 × 6)  Step 1: Break up the divisor into a
                          basic multiplication fact. These
                          numbers will become the divisors
                          for the next steps.
= (2,880 ÷ 4) ÷ 6  Step 2: Divide the dividend by the first
                          divisor.
= 720 ÷ 6       Step 3: Divide the number obtained in
= **120**          Step 2 by the second divisor.

**17 Division: Finding Remainders When Dividing by 5**

Find the remainder of 7,429 ÷ 5.

7,429 ÷ 5         ❑ Divide the last digit of the dividend by
9 ÷ 5 = 1 R **4**     5 to find the remainder.
The remainder of 7,429 ÷ 5 is **4**.

**18 Division: Finding Remainders When Dividing by 8**

Find the remainder of 4,169 ÷ 8.

4,169 ÷ 8         ❑ Divide the last three digits of the
                dividend by 8 to find the
169 ÷ 8 = 21 R **1**   remainder.
The remainder of 4,169 ÷ 8 is **1**.

**19 Division: Finding Remainders When Dividing by 9**

Find the remainder of 9,478 ÷ 9.

9 + 4 + 7 + 8 = 28  ❑ Add all four digits of the dividend.
2 + 8 = 10        ❑ Add until the number becomes a
1 + 0 = **1**         single digit.
The remainder of 9,478 ÷ 9 is **1**.

**21 Division: Dividing Numbers by 25**

7,000 ÷ 25
7,000 ÷ 25 = (7,000 × 4) ÷ 100  ❑ Multiply the dividend and the
                        divisor by 4.
= 28,000 ÷ 100     ❑ Divide the product by 100 to find
= **280**           the answer.

**22 Adding Fractions with Unlike Denominators**

$\frac{1}{10} + \frac{5}{6}$

Step 1: To find the numerator of the answer,

$\frac{1}{10} \diagup\!\!\!\!\diagdown \frac{5}{6}$
(5 × 10)   (1 × 6)    ❑ Cross multiply the numerators by the
                denominators. Add the products.

50 + 6 = 56

Step 2: To find the denominator of the answer,
10 × 6 = 60       ❑ Multiply both denominators.
$\frac{1}{10} + \frac{5}{6} = \frac{\textbf{56}}{\textbf{60}}$

**23 Subtracting Fractions with Unlike Denominators**

$\frac{4}{9} - \frac{1}{5}$

Step 1: To find the numerator of the answer,

$\frac{4}{9} \diagup\!\!\!\!\diagdown \frac{1}{5}$
(4 × 5)   (1 × 9)    ❑ Cross multiply the numerators by the
                denominators. Subtract the products.

20 − 9 = 11

Step 2: To find the denominator of the answer,
9 × 5 = 45        ❑ Multiply both denominators.
$\frac{4}{9} - \frac{1}{5} = \frac{\textbf{11}}{\textbf{45}}$

## 24 Multiplying Fractions and Whole Numbers

$5\frac{1}{7} \times 28$

$5\frac{1}{7} = 5 + \frac{1}{7}$

❑ Break up the mixed number by separating the whole number and the fraction.

$(5 + \frac{1}{7}) \times 28 = (5 \times 28) + (\frac{1}{7} \times 28)$

❑ Multiply the whole number and the fraction by the whole number factor.

$= 140 + 4$
$= 144$

❑ Add the products to find the answer.

$5\frac{1}{7} \times 28 = \textbf{144}$

## 26 Multiplying Identical Mixed Numbers with the Fraction $\frac{1}{2}$

$2\frac{1}{2} \times 2\frac{1}{2}$

$(2 + \frac{1}{2}) \times (2 + \frac{1}{2})$

Step 1: Break up the mixed numbers.

$2 \times (2 + 1)$
$= 2 \times 3$
$= 6$

Step 2: Multiply the whole number by the number one more than itself.

$\frac{1}{2} \times \frac{1}{2} = \frac{1}{4}$

Step 3: Multiply the fractions.

$2\frac{1}{2} \times 2\frac{1}{2} = \textbf{6}\frac{1}{4}$

Step 4: Combine the whole number obtained in Step 2 with the fraction obtained in Step 3.

## 27 Multiplying Mixed Numbers with Identical Fractions When the Numerator Is 1

$3\frac{1}{6} \times 9\frac{1}{6}$

$(3 + \frac{1}{6}) \times (9 + \frac{1}{6})$

Step 1: Break up the mixed numbers.

$(3 + 9) \div 6 = 12 \div 6$
$= 2$

Step 2: Add the two whole numbers and divide the sum by the common denominator.

$(3 \times 9) + 2 = 27 + 2$
$= 29$

Step 3: Multiply the two whole numbers. Add the product to the quotient obtained in Step 2.

$\frac{1}{6} \times \frac{1}{6} = \frac{1}{36}$

Step 4: Multiply the fractions.

$3\frac{1}{6} \times 9\frac{1}{6} = \textbf{29}\frac{1}{36}$

Step 5: Combine the whole number obtained in Step 3 with the fraction obtained in Step 4.

## 28 Multiplying Mixed Numbers with Identical Whole Numbers

$6\frac{1}{4} \times 6\frac{3}{4}$

$(6 + \frac{1}{4}) \times (6 + \frac{3}{4})$

Step 1: Break up the mixed numbers.

$6 \times (6 + 1) = 6 \times 7$
$= 42$

Step 2: Multiply the whole number by the number one more than itself.

$\frac{1}{4} \times \frac{3}{4} = \frac{3}{16}$

Step 3: Multiply the fractions.

$6\frac{1}{4} \times 6\frac{3}{4} = \textbf{42}\frac{3}{16}$

Step 4: Combine the whole number obtained in Step 2 with the fraction obtained in Step 3.

## 29 Dividing Fractions by Whole Numbers

$\frac{25}{60} \div 5$

$\frac{(25 \div 5)}{60} = \frac{5}{60}$

❑ Divide the numerator by the divisor. The denominator remains the same.

$\frac{5}{60} = \frac{(5 \div 5)}{(60 \div 5)} = \frac{1}{12}$

❑ Simplify the fraction to the lowest term.

## 31 Converting Fractions to Percentages

Convert $\frac{7}{25}$ to a percentage.

$100 \div 25 = 4$

❑ Divide 100 by the denominator.

$4 \times 7 = 28$

❑ Multiply the quotient by the numerator to find the answer.

$\frac{7}{25} = \textbf{28\%}$

## 32 Percentage: 5% of a Number

Find 5% of 280.

$280 \div 10 = 28$

❑ Divide the number by 10.

$28 \div 2 = 14$

❑ Divide the quotient by 2 to find the answer.

5% of 280 = **14**

## 33 Percentage: 15% of a Number

Find 15% of 550.

$550 \div 10 = 55$

Step 1: Divide the number by 10.

$55 \div 2 = 27.5$

Step 2: Divide the quotient by 2.

$55 + 27.5 = 82.5$

Step 3: Add the quotients obtained in Steps 1 and 2.

15% of 550 = **82.5**

## 34 Percentage: 20% of a Number

Find 20% of 630.

$630 \div 5 = 126$

❑ Divide the number by 5 to find the answer.

20% of 630 = **126**

## 36 Percentage: 45% of a Number

Find 45% of 300.

$300 \div 20 = 15$

❑ Divide the number by 20.

$15 \times 9 = 135$

❑ Multiply the quotient by 9 to find the answer.

45% of 300 = **135**

## 37 Squaring Numbers Ending with 5

Find the value of $15^2$.

Step 1: To find the first few digits of the answer,

$1 \times (1 + 1) = 1 \times 2$
$= 2$

❑ Multiply the tens digit of the number by the number one more than itself.

Step 2: To find the last two digits of the answer,

$5 \times 5 = \textbf{25}$

❑ Multiply the ones digit of the number by itself.

$15^2 = \textbf{225}$

## 38 Squaring Numbers Beginning with 9

Find the value of $91^2$.

Step 1: To find the first few digits of the answer,

$100 - 91 = 9$
$100 - 9 - 9 = \textbf{82}$

❑ Subtract the number from 100. Subtract the difference from 100 twice.

Step 2: To find the last two digits of the answer,

$9 \times 9 = \textbf{81}$

❑ Multiply the difference obtained in Step 1 by itself.

$91^2 = \textbf{8,281}$

## 39 Squaring Numbers Ending with 7

Find the value of $87^2$.

Step 1: To find the last digit of the answer,

$7 \times 7 = 4\textcircled{9}$

❑ Multiply the ones digit by itself.

Step 2: To find the next-to-last digit of the answer,

$(8 + 1) \times 4$
$= 9 \times 4$
$= 3\textcircled{6}$

❑ Add 1 to the tens digit of the number. Multiply the sum by 4. Carry the tens digit of the product to the next step.

Step 3: To find the first few digits of the answer,

$8 \times (8 + 1) + 3$
$= (8 \times 9) + 3$
$= 72 + 3$
$= \textbf{75}$

❑ Multiply the tens digit by the number one more than itself. Add the digit carried from Step 2.

$87^2 = \textbf{7,569}$

## 41 Squaring Numbers Ending with 8

Find the value of $98^2$.

Step 1: To find the last digit of the answer,

$8 \times 8 = 6\textcircled{4}$

❑ Multiply the ones digit by itself.

Step 2: To find the next-to-last digit of the answer,

$(9 + 1) \times 6$
$= 10 \times 6$
$= 6\textcircled{0}$

❑ Add 1 to the tens digit of the number. Multiply the sum by 6. Carry the tens digit of the product to the next step.

Step 3: To find the first few digits of the answer,

$9 \times (9 + 1) + 6$
$= (9 \times 10) + 6$
$= 90 + 6$
$= \textbf{96}$

❑ Multiply the tens digit by the number one more than itself. Add the digit carried from Step 2.

$98^2 = \textbf{9,604}$

## 42 Squaring Numbers Ending with 9

Find the value of $29^2$.

Step 1: To find the last digit of the answer,

$9 \times 9 = 8\textcircled{1}$

❑ Multiply the ones digit by itself.

Step 2: To find the next-to-last digit of the answer,

$(2 + 1) \times 8$
$= 3 \times 8$
$= 2\textcircled{4}$

❑ Add 1 to the tens digit of the number. Multiply the sum by 8. Carry the tens digit of the product to the next step.

Step 3: To find the first few digits of the answer,

$2 \times (2 + 1) + 2$
$= (2 \times 3) + 2$
$= 6 + 2$
$= \textbf{8}$

❑ Multiply the tens digit by the number one more than itself. Add the digit carried from Step 2.

$29^2 = \textbf{841}$

## 43 Squaring Numbers from 40 to 50

Find the value of $44^2$.

Step 1: To find the last two digits of the answer,

$50 - 44 = 6$
$6 \times 6 = \textbf{36}$

❑ Subtract the number from 50. Multiply the difference by itself.

Step 2: To find the first two digits of the answer,

$25 - 6 = \textbf{19}$
$44^2 = \textbf{1,936}$

❑ Subtract the difference obtained in Step 1 from 25.

## 44 Adding a Series of Consecutive Numbers

$1 + 2 + 3 + 4 + ... + 10$

$10 \times (10 + 1)$
$= 10 \times 11$
$= 110$

❑ Multiply the last number in the series by the number one more than itself.

$110 \div 2 = 55$
$1 + 2 + 3 + 4 + 5 + 6 + 7 + 8 + 9 + 10 = \textbf{55}$

❑ Divide the product by 2 to find the answer.

## 45 Adding a Series of Numbers

$1 + 2 + 3 + 4 + 5 + 4 + 3 + 2 + 1$

$5^2 = 25$

❑ Square the largest number in the series to find the answer.

$1 + 2 + 3 + 4 + 5 + 4 + 3 + 2 + 1 = \textbf{25}$

# STRATEGY

## Addition: Rounding Large Numbers Beginning with 9

**Strategy**

Find the value of 999,900 + 999,800

999,900 ≈ 1,000,000
(999,900 + 100)
999,800 ≈ 1,000,000
(999,800 + 200)
999,900 + 999,800
= (1,000,000 + 1,000,000) – 200 – 100
= (2,000,000 – 200) – 100

= 1,999,800 – 100
= **1,999,700**

Step 1: Round each number up to the nearest million.

Step 2: Add the millions. Subtract the amount needed to round up in Step 1 from the sum.

Step 3: Subtract to find the answer.

**Solve each problem mentally.**

1. 999,992 + 999,999 =

2. 9,999,991 + 9,999,899 =

3. 999,000 + 999,000 =

4. 999,890 + 999,700 =

5. 999,800 + 999,999 =

6. 9,999,889 + 9,999,998 =

7. 9,999,780 + 9,999,840 =

8. 9,999,898 + 9,999,600 =

9. 999,899 + 999,799 =

10. 9,999,998 + 9,999,888 =

STRATEGY

## Addition: Breaking Up Numbers

**Strategy**

Find the value of 699,000 + 101,000.

699,000 + 101,000
= (690,000 + 100,000) + (9,000 + 1,000)  ❑ Break up and arrange the numbers for easy addition.

= 790,000 + 10,000  ❑ Add the numbers to find the answer.
= **800,000**

**Solve each problem mentally.**

1.  58,350 + 19,650 =

2.  145,046 + 308,244 =

3.  800,125 + 250,875 =

4.  693,025 + 488,075 =

5.  499,700 + 100,300 =

6.  534,550 + 612,450 =

7.  489,901 + 710,099 =

8.  908,808 + 89,812 =

9.  753,800 + 122,200 =

10.  394,600 + 400,400 =

# WEEK 3 STRATEGY

## Subtraction: Breaking Up Numbers

**Strategy**

Find the value of 199,980 − 99,800.

199,980 − 99,800
= (199,800 + 180) − 99,800
= 199,800 − 99,800 + 180
= 100,000 + 180
= **100,180**

❑ Break up the first number for easy subtraction.

❑ Subtract the larger numbers. Add the remaining number to the difference to find the answer.

**Solve each problem mentally.**

1. 699,992 − 99,988 =

2. 499,990 − 199,890 =

3. 699,989 − 399,890 =

4. 899,930 − 699,880 =

5. 399,999 − 299,800 =

6. 799,950 − 499,890 =

7. 999,999 − 599,899 =

8. 29,999 − 19,889 =

9. 59,999 − 49,897 =

10. 399,986 − 89,893 =

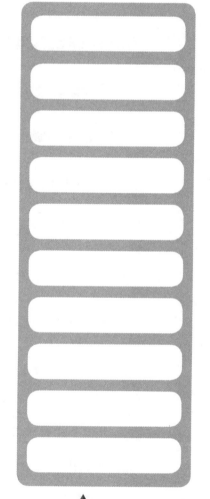

STRATEGY

## Subtraction: Reverse Three-Digit Numbers

**Strategy**

Find the value of 895 − 598.

8 − 5 = 3    Step 1: Find the difference of the hundreds digits in both numbers.

3 × 100 = 300    Step 2: Multiply the difference obtained in Step 1 by 100.

300 − 3 = 297    Step 3: Subtract the difference obtained in Step 1 from the product obtained in Step 2.

895 − 598 = **297**

**Solve each problem mentally.**

1. 932 − 239 =

2. 983 − 389 =

3. 652 − 256 =

4. 504 − 405 =

5. 951 − 159 =

6. 742 − 247 =

7. 312 − 213 =

8. 957 − 759 =

9. 862 − 268 =

10. 641 − 146 =

# GENERAL REVIEW 1

**Solve each problem mentally.**

1. 9,999,987 + 9,999,888 =

2. 896 – 698 =

3. 488,988 + 100,012 =

4. 9,999,898 + 9,999,986 =

5. 599,999 – 199,088 =

6. 399,989 – 99,981 =

7. 716 – 617 =

8. 999,885 + 999,995 =

9. 941 – 149 =

10. 91,462 + 13,038 =

# WEEK 6 STRATEGY

## Rearranging to Multiply by 100

**Strategy**

Find the value of 25 × 89 × 4.

25 × 89 × 4 = 89 × 25 × 4

             = 89 × 100
             = **8,900**

❑ Arrange the numbers to create the factor 100.
❑ Multiply the remaining factor by 100 to find the answer.

**Solve each problem mentally.**

**1.** 50 × 39 × 2 =

**2.** 20 × 77 × 5 =

**3.** 5 × 55 × 20 =

**4.** 25 × 96 × 4 =

**5.** 2 × 48 × 50 =

**6.** 4 × 64 × 25 =

**7.** 20 × 26 × 5 =

**8.** 50 × 19 × 2 =

**9.** 25 × 52 × 4 =

**10.** 5 × 33 × 20 =

# Rearranging to Multiply by 1,000

**Strategy**

Find the value of 125 × 860 × 8.

125 × 860 × 8 = 860 × 125 × 8

❑ Arrange the numbers to create the factor 1,000.

= 860 × 1,000

❑ Multiply the remaining factor by 1,000 to find the answer.

= **860,000**

**Solve each problem mentally.**

1.  50 × 213 × 20 =

2.  4 × 743 × 250 =

3.  125 × 316 × 8 =

4.  200 × 976 × 5 =

5.  8 × 628 × 125 =

6.  250 × 816 × 4 =

7.  20 × 511 × 50 =

8.  50 × 177 × 20 =

9.  125 × 401 × 8 =

10. 5 × 837 × 200 =

# 8 STRATEGY

## Double the 50

**Strategy**

Find the value of 68 × 50.

$$68 \times 50 = 68 \times 100 \div 2$$
$$= 68 \div 2 \times 100$$
$$= 34 \times 100$$
$$= \mathbf{3,400}$$

❑ Replace the factor 50 with 100 ÷ 2.

❑ Arrange the equation. Divide the first factor by 2. Multiply the quotient by 100 to find the answer.

**Solve each problem mentally.**

**1.** 44 × 50 =

**2.** 37 × 50 =

**3.** 19 × 50 =

**4.** 28 × 50 =

**5.** 66 × 50 =

**6.** 93 × 50 =

**7.** 84 × 50 =

**8.** 71 × 50 =

**9.** 53 × 50 =

**10.** 99 × 50 =

# STRATEGY

## Multiplying Four-Digit Numbers by 11

**Strategy**

Find the value of 5,243 × 11.

Step 1: The first and last digits of the number will be the first and last digits of the answer.

First digit of the answer: **5**
Last digit of the answer: **3**

Step 2: To find the middle three digits, start with the left and add each digit to the digit next to it.

| first digit | | | | last digit |
|---|---|---|---|---|
| 5 | (5 + 2) | (2 + 4) | (4 + 3) | 3 |
| 5 | 7 | 6 | 7 | 3 |

5,243 × 11 = **57,673**

Note: This strategy only works when there is no regrouping in Step 2.

**Solve each problem mentally.**

1.  1,234 × 11 =

2.  3,031 × 11 =

3.  4,522 × 11 =

4.  4,523 × 11 =

5.  6,324 × 11 =

6.  2,527 × 11 =

7.  5,316 × 11 =

8.  3,634 × 11 =

9.  7,027 × 11 =

10.  3,453 × 11 =

## GENERAL REVIEW 2

**Solve each problem mentally.**

1. $50 \times 43 \times 2 =$

2. $88 \times 50 =$

3. $250 \times 716 \times 4 =$

4. $6,132 \times 11 =$

5. $4 \times 81 \times 25 =$

6. $1,417 \times 11 =$

7. $25 \times 18 \times 4 =$

8. $56 \times 50 =$

9. $2,424 \times 11 =$

10. $125 \times 35 \times 8 =$

## STRATEGY

## Multiplying Numbers by 12

**Strategy**

Find the value of 58 × 12.

58 × 12 = (50 × 12) + (8 × 12)    ❑ Expand the first factor. Multiply both parts by 12.

        = 600 + 96    ❑ Add the products to find the answer.

        = **696**

**Solve each problem mentally.**

**1.** 38 × 12 =

**2.** 69 × 12 =

**3.** 43 × 12 =

**4.** 54 × 12 =

**5.** 82 × 12 =

**6.** 75 × 12 =

**7.** 91 × 12 =

**8.** 18 × 12 =

**9.** 48 × 12 =

**10.** 29 × 12 =

# STRATEGY

## Multiplying Numbers by 15

**Strategy**

Find the value of 78 × 15.

78 × 15 = (78 × 10) + (78 × 5)

   = 780 + 390

   = **1,170**

❏ Expand 15 into 10 and 5. Multiply the first factor by both 10 and 5.

❏ Add the products to find the answer.

**Solve each problem mentally.**

1. 45 × 15 =

2. 29 × 15 =

3. 67 × 15 =

4. 92 × 15 =

5. 34 × 15 =

6. 17 × 15 =

7. 86 × 15 =

8. 21 × 15 =

9. 90 × 15 =

10. 73 × 15 =

# WEEK 13

## STRATEGY

### Multiplying Numbers by 25

**Strategy**

Find the value of 63 × 25.

63 × (25 × 4)

= (63 × 100) ÷ 4

= 6,300 ÷ 4

= **1,575**

❑ Multiply 25 by 4 to make 100.
❑ Find the product and divide by 4 to find the answer.

**Solve each problem mentally.**

1. 31 × 25 =

2. 22 × 25 =

3. 44 × 25 =

4. 93 × 25 =

5. 37 × 25 =

6. 12 × 25 =

7. 63 × 25 =

8. 52 × 25 =

9. 87 × 25 =

10. 74 × 25 =

20

WEEK **14**

## STRATEGY

## Multiplying Numbers by 50

**Strategy**

Find the value of 57 × 50.

57 × (50 × 2)

= (57 × 100) ÷ 2

= 5,700 ÷ 2

= **2,850**

❏ Multiply 50 by 2 to make 100.

❏ Find the product and divide by 2 to find the answer.

**Solve each problem mentally.**

**1.** 36 × 50 =

**2.** 17 × 50 =

**3.** 48 × 50 =

**4.** 63 × 50 =

**5.** 94 × 50 =

**6.** 29 × 50 =

**7.** 55 × 50 =

**8.** 78 × 50 =

**9.** 81 × 50 =

**10.** 69 × 50 =

## GENERAL REVIEW 3

**Solve each problem mentally.**

1.  40 × 12 =

2.  77 × 15 =

3.  38 × 25 =

4.  56 × 12 =

5.  53 × 50 =

6.  89 × 12 =

7.  31 × 15 =

8.  72 × 25 =

9.  18 × 15 =

10. 61 × 50 =

## STRATEGY

### Division: Breaking Up Divisors

**Strategy**

Find the value of 2,880 ÷ 24.

2,880 ÷ 24 = 2,880 ÷ (4 × 6)    Step 1: Break up the divisor into a basic multiplication fact. These numbers will become the divisors for the next steps.

= (2,880 ÷ 4) ÷ 6    Step 2: Divide the dividend by the first divisor.

= 720 ÷ 6    Step 3: Divide the number obtained in

= **120**    Step 2 by the second divisor.

Helpful Hint: This strategy works best when using mastered basic multiplication facts.

**Solve each problem mentally.**

**1.** 1,620 ÷ 18 =

**2.** 2,400 ÷ 25 =

**3.** 3,996 ÷ 36 =

**4.** 3,800 ÷ 40 =

**5.** 4,452 ÷ 42 =

**6.** 5,208 ÷ 24 =

**7.** 4,704 ÷ 56 =

**8.** 7,744 ÷ 64 =

**9.** 4,263 ÷ 49 =

**10.** 5,096 ÷ 28 =

# WEEK 17

## STRATEGY

### Division: Finding Remainders When Dividing by 5

**Strategy**

Find the remainder of 7,429 ÷ 5.

7,429 ÷ 5
9 ÷ 5 = 1 R **4**
The remainder of 7,429 ÷ 5 is **4**.

❑ Divide the last digit of the dividend by 5 to find the remainder.

Note: If the last digit of the dividend is less than 5, divide the last two digits of the dividend by 5. (For 7,431 ÷ 5, use 31 ÷ 5.)

**Find each remainder mentally.**

1. 8,524 ÷ 5    R =

2. 6,933 ÷ 5    R =

3. 7,008 ÷ 5    R =

4. 5,807 ÷ 5    R =

5. 3,349 ÷ 5    R =

6. 2,892 ÷ 5    R =

7. 9,976 ÷ 5    R =

8. 1,846 ÷ 5    R =

9. 7,943 ÷ 5    R =

10. 4,386 ÷ 5    R =

## STRATEGY

### Division: Finding Remainders When Dividing by 8

**Strategy**

Find the remainder of $4,169 \div 8$.

$4,169 \div 8$

❑ Divide the last three digits of the dividend by 8 to find the remainder.

$169 \div 8 = 21$ R **1**

The remainder of $4,169 \div 8$ is **1**.

**Find each remainder mentally.**

**1.** $9,415 \div 8$    R =

**2.** $3,235 \div 8$    R =

**3.** $1,097 \div 8$    R =

**4.** $4,455 \div 8$    R =

**5.** $6,361 \div 8$    R =

**6.** $8,706 \div 8$    R =

**7.** $2,948 \div 8$    R =

**8.** $5,742 \div 8$    R =

**9.** $7,545 \div 8$    R =

**10.** $3,678 \div 8$    R =

# STRATEGY

## Division: Finding Remainders When Dividing by 9

**Strategy**

Find the remainder of 9,478 ÷ 9.

9 + 4 + 7 + 8 = 28

2 + 8 = 10

1 + 0 = **1**

The remainder of 9,478 ÷ 9 is **1**.

❑ Add all four digits of the dividend.

❑ Add until the number becomes a single digit.

**Find each remainder mentally.**

**1.** 8,345 ÷ 9    R =

**2.** 1,889 ÷ 9    R =

**3.** 6,302 ÷ 9    R =

**4.** 4,126 ÷ 9    R =

**5.** 5,183 ÷ 9    R =

**6.** 7,633 ÷ 9    R =

**7.** 3,491 ÷ 9    R =

**8.** 9,807 ÷ 9    R =

**9.** 2,864 ÷ 9    R =

**10.** 6,879 ÷ 9    R =

# GENERAL REVIEW 4

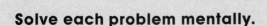

**Solve each problem mentally.**

**1.** 3,220 ÷ 35 =

**2.** Find the remainder of 8,637 ÷ 5.

R =

**3.** Find the remainder of 4,263 ÷ 8.

R =

**4.** Find the remainder of 7,541 ÷ 9.

R =

**5.** 1,755 ÷ 27 =

**6.** 5,544 ÷ 63 =

**7.** Find the remainder of 2,973 ÷ 9.

R =

**8.** 2,190 ÷ 30 =

**9.** Find the remainder of 6,849 ÷ 8.

R =

**10.** Find the remainder of 1,094 ÷ 5.

R =

STRATEGY

## Division: Dividing Numbers by 25

**Strategy**

Find the value of $7,000 \div 25$.

$7,000 \div 25 = (7,000 \times 4) \div 100$    ❑ Multiply the dividend and the divisor by 4.

$\qquad\qquad = 28,000 \div 100$    ❑ Divide the product by 100 to find the answer.

$\qquad\qquad = \mathbf{280}$

Note: The last digit or digits in the dividend must be 0, 50, or 75 for this strategy to work.

**Solve each problem mentally.**

1.   $1,200 \div 25 =$

2.   $9,075 \div 25 =$

3.   $2,150 \div 25 =$

4.   $8,400 \div 25 =$

5.   $5,225 \div 25 =$

6.   $6,250 \div 25 =$

7.   $7,850 \div 25 =$

8.   $4,075 \div 25 =$

9.   $3,725 \div 25 =$

10.   $8,550 \div 25 =$

# WEEK 22 STRATEGY

## Adding Fractions with Unlike Denominators

**Strategy**

Find the value of $\frac{1}{10} + \frac{5}{6}$.

Step 1: To find the numerator of the answer,

$$\frac{1}{10} \times \frac{5}{6}$$
$$(5 \times 10) \qquad (1 \times 6)$$

❑ Cross multiply the numerators by the denominators. Add the products.

$$50 + 6 = 56$$

Step 2: To find the denominator of the answer,

$$10 \times 6 = 60$$

❑ Multiply both denominators.

$$\frac{1}{10} + \frac{5}{6} = \frac{56}{60}$$

**Solve each problem mentally. Do not simplify to lowest terms.**

1. $\frac{1}{4} + \frac{5}{8} =$

2. $\frac{2}{5} + \frac{7}{12} =$

3. $\frac{1}{2} + \frac{2}{3} =$

4. $\frac{3}{7} + \frac{1}{4} =$

5. $\frac{1}{6} + \frac{3}{7} =$

6. $\frac{3}{4} + \frac{5}{9} =$

7. $\frac{4}{11} + \frac{6}{12} =$

8. $\frac{6}{10} + \frac{7}{9} =$

9. $\frac{5}{8} + \frac{2}{6} =$

10. $\frac{6}{7} + \frac{5}{9} =$

## Subtracting Fractions with Unlike Denominators

**Strategy**

Find the value of $\frac{4}{9} - \frac{1}{5}$.

Step 1: To find the numerator of the answer,

$$\frac{4}{9} \times \frac{1}{5}$$

$(4 \times 5) \qquad (1 \times 9)$

❑ Cross multiply the numerators by the denominators. Subtract the products.

$20 - 9 = 11$

Step 2: To find the denominator of the answer,

$9 \times 5 = 45$ ❑ Multiply both denominators.

$$\frac{4}{9} - \frac{1}{5} = \frac{11}{45}$$

**Solve each problem mentally. Do not simplify to lowest terms.**

1. $\frac{3}{7} - \frac{2}{5} =$

2. $\frac{7}{8} - \frac{2}{6} =$

3. $\frac{4}{5} - \frac{2}{3} =$

4. $\frac{7}{12} - \frac{1}{3} =$

5. $\frac{5}{9} - \frac{2}{7} =$

6. $\frac{4}{5} - \frac{1}{2} =$

7. $\frac{9}{10} - \frac{5}{6} =$

8. $\frac{8}{12} - \frac{3}{11} =$

9. $\frac{5}{9} - \frac{1}{10} =$

10. $\frac{2}{3} - \frac{1}{4} =$

# 24
## STRATEGY

### ● ● ● Multiplying Fractions and Whole Numbers ● ● ●

**Strategy**

Find the value of $5\frac{1}{7} \times 28$.

$5\frac{1}{7} = 5 + \frac{1}{7}$

$(5 + \frac{1}{7}) \times 28 = (5 \times 28) + (\frac{1}{7} \times 28)$

$= 140 + 4$
$= 144$

$5\frac{1}{7} \times 28 = \mathbf{144}$

Note: $\frac{1}{7} \times 28 = \frac{28}{7} = 28 \div 7 = 4$

❑ Break up the mixed number by separating the whole number and the fraction.

❑ Multiply the whole number and the fraction by the whole number factor.

❑ Add the products to find the answer.

**Solve each problem mentally. Do not simplify to lowest terms.**

1. $3\frac{1}{6} \times 18 =$

2. $4\frac{3}{5} \times 15 =$

3. $1\frac{2}{11} \times 22 =$

4. $5\frac{3}{8} \times 8 =$

5. $8\frac{2}{3} \times 9 =$

6. $9\frac{2}{3} \times 6 =$

7. $7\frac{2}{5} \times 15 =$

8. $11\frac{2}{9} \times 18 =$

9. $2\frac{3}{7} \times 14 =$

10. $6\frac{3}{4} \times 8 =$

31

# GENERAL REVIEW 5

**Solve each problem mentally. Do not simplify to lowest terms.**

1.  $\dfrac{2}{5} + \dfrac{1}{6} =$

2.  $\dfrac{7}{8} - \dfrac{6}{9} =$

3.  $\dfrac{9}{11} - \dfrac{1}{2} =$

4.  $10\dfrac{1}{5} \times 30 =$

5.  $8,125 \div 25 =$

6.  $\dfrac{1}{9} + \dfrac{5}{11} =$

7.  $12\dfrac{3}{4} \times 16 =$

8.  $3,425 \div 25 =$

9.  $8\dfrac{1}{7} \times 49 =$

10. $9,075 \div 25 =$

STRATEGY

## Multiplying Identical Mixed Numbers with the Fraction $\frac{1}{2}$

**Strategy**

Find the value of $2\frac{1}{2} \times 2\frac{1}{2}$.

$(2 + \frac{1}{2}) \times (2 + \frac{1}{2})$      Step 1: Break up the mixed numbers.

$2 \times (2 + 1)$      Step 2: Multiply the whole number by the
$= 2 \times 3$                    number one more than itself.
$= 6$

$\frac{1}{2} \times \frac{1}{2} = \frac{1}{4}$      Step 3: Multiply the fractions.

$2\frac{1}{2} \times 2\frac{1}{2} = \mathbf{6\frac{1}{4}}$      Step 4: Combine the whole number
                            obtained in Step 2 with the fraction
                            obtained in Step 3.

**Solve each problem mentally.**

1.   $1\frac{1}{2} \times 1\frac{1}{2} =$

2.   $4\frac{1}{2} \times 4\frac{1}{2} =$

3.   $6\frac{1}{2} \times 6\frac{1}{2} =$

4.   $5\frac{1}{2} \times 5\frac{1}{2} =$

5.   $3\frac{1}{2} \times 3\frac{1}{2} =$

6.   $8\frac{1}{2} \times 8\frac{1}{2} =$

7.   $10\frac{1}{2} \times 10\frac{1}{2} =$

8.   $12\frac{1}{2} \times 12\frac{1}{2} =$

9.   $9\frac{1}{2} \times 9\frac{1}{2} =$

10.   $7\frac{1}{2} \times 7\frac{1}{2} =$

## Multiplying Mixed Numbers with Identical Fractions When the Numerator Is 1

**Strategy**

Find the value of $3\frac{1}{6} \times 9\frac{1}{6}$.

$(3 + \frac{1}{6}) \times (9 + \frac{1}{6})$     Step 1: Break up the mixed numbers.

$\begin{aligned}(3 + 9) \div 6 &= 12 \div 6\\ &= 2\end{aligned}$     Step 2: Add the two whole numbers and divide the sum by the denominator.

$\begin{aligned}(3 \times 9) + 2 &= 27 + 2\\ &= 29\end{aligned}$     Step 3: Multiply the two whole numbers. Add the product to the quotient obtained in Step 2.

$\frac{1}{6} \times \frac{1}{6} = \frac{1}{36}$     Step 4: Multiply the fractions.

$3\frac{1}{6} \times 9\frac{1}{6} = \mathbf{29\frac{1}{36}}$     Step 5: Combine the whole number obtained in Step 3 with the fraction obtained in Step 4.

Note: This strategy only works when the numerator of the fraction is 1.

**Solve each problem mentally.**

1. $5\frac{1}{4} \times 3\frac{1}{4} =$

2. $9\frac{1}{3} \times 3\frac{1}{3} =$

3. $10\frac{1}{5} \times 20\frac{1}{5} =$

4. $8\frac{1}{4} \times 4\frac{1}{4} =$

5. $7\frac{1}{10} \times 3\frac{1}{10} =$

6. $12\frac{1}{2} \times 10\frac{1}{2} =$

7. $8\frac{1}{2} \times 6\frac{1}{2} =$

8. $11\frac{1}{7} \times 3\frac{1}{7} =$

9. $6\frac{1}{9} \times 3\frac{1}{9} =$

10. $12\frac{1}{5} \times 8\frac{1}{5} =$

## STRATEGY

## Multiplying Mixed Numbers with Identical Whole Numbers

**Strategy**

Find the value of $6\frac{1}{4} \times 6\frac{3}{4}$.

$(6 + \frac{1}{4}) \times (6 + \frac{3}{4})$      Step 1: Break up the mixed numbers.

$6 \times (6 + 1) = 6 \times 7$
$\qquad\qquad\quad = 42$      Step 2: Multiply the whole number by the number one more than itself.

$\frac{1}{4} \times \frac{3}{4} = \frac{3}{16}$      Step 3: Multiply the fractions.

$6\frac{1}{4} \times 6\frac{3}{4} = \mathbf{42\frac{3}{16}}$      Step 4: Combine the whole number obtained in Step 2 with the fraction obtained in Step 3.

Note: This strategy only works when the sum of the two fractions is 1.

**Solve each problem mentally. Do not simplify to lowest terms.**

1.   $10\frac{1}{3} \times 10\frac{2}{3} =$

2.   $4\frac{2}{5} \times 4\frac{3}{5} =$

3.   $7\frac{4}{7} \times 7\frac{3}{7} =$

4.   $3\frac{1}{9} \times 3\frac{8}{9} =$

5.   $5\frac{2}{3} \times 5\frac{1}{3} =$

6.   $8\frac{4}{6} \times 8\frac{2}{6} =$

7.   $9\frac{7}{10} \times 9\frac{3}{10} =$

8.   $6\frac{1}{6} \times 6\frac{5}{6} =$

9.   $11\frac{2}{8} \times 11\frac{6}{8} =$

10.   $2\frac{5}{12} \times 2\frac{7}{12} =$

## Dividing Fractions by Whole Numbers

**Strategy**

Find the value of $\frac{25}{60} \div 5$.

$\frac{(25 \div 5)}{60} = \frac{5}{60}$

$\frac{5}{60} = \frac{(5 \div 5)}{(60 \div 5)} = \frac{1}{12}$

❑ Divide the numerator by the divisor. The denominator remains the same.
❑ Simplify the fraction to the lowest term.

**Solve each problem mentally.**

1. $\frac{16}{24} \div 8 =$

2. $\frac{27}{50} \div 9 =$

3. $\frac{12}{15} \div 3 =$

4. $\frac{39}{36} \div 13 =$

5. $\frac{15}{25} \div 5 =$

6. $\frac{18}{20} \div 6 =$

7. $\frac{32}{40} \div 4 =$

8. $\frac{42}{100} \div 7 =$

9. $\frac{10}{12} \div 2 =$

10. $\frac{55}{22} \div 11 =$

# GENERAL REVIEW 6

**Solve each problem mentally.**

1. $11\dfrac{1}{2} \times 11\dfrac{1}{2} =$

2. $4\dfrac{1}{6} \times 8\dfrac{1}{6} =$

3. $11\dfrac{2}{5} \times 11\dfrac{3}{5} =$

4. $\dfrac{60}{80} \div 5 =$

5. $10\dfrac{1}{11} \times 12\dfrac{1}{11} =$

6. $15\dfrac{1}{2} \times 15\dfrac{1}{2} =$

7. $9\dfrac{4}{7} \times 9\dfrac{3}{7} =$

8. $\dfrac{72}{96} \div 12 =$

9. $13\dfrac{1}{9} \times 5\dfrac{1}{9} =$

10. $\dfrac{32}{48} \div 8 =$

## Converting Fractions to Percentages

**Strategy**

Convert $\frac{7}{25}$ to a percentage.

$100 \div 25 = 4$

$4 \times 7 = 28$

$\frac{7}{25} = \textbf{28\%}$

❏ Divide 100 by the denominator.

❏ Multiply the quotient by the numerator to find the answer.

**Convert each fraction to a percentage mentally.**

1. $\frac{9}{20} =$

2. $\frac{13}{50} =$

3. $\frac{5}{10} =$

4. $\frac{13}{25} =$

5. $\frac{16}{20} =$

6. $\frac{29}{50} =$

7. $\frac{15}{25} =$

8. $\frac{3}{4} =$

9. $\frac{3}{5} =$

10. $\frac{1}{2} =$

38

# 32

## STRATEGY

## Percentage: 5% of a Number

**Strategy**

Find 5% of 280.

$280 \div 10 = 28$    ❑ Divide the number by 10.

$28 \div 2 = 14$    ❑ Divide the quotient by 2 to find the answer.

5% of 280 = **14**

Helpful Hint: This strategy can be solved in one step when you divide the number by 20. ($280 \div 20 = $ **14**)

**Find each percentage mentally.**

1.   5% of 140 =

2.   5% of 220 =

3.   5% of 350 =

4.   5% of 460 =

5.   5% of 550 =

6.   5% of 960 =

7.   5% of 710 =

8.   5% of 618 =

9.   5% of 1,230 =

10.   5% of 2,462 =

STRATEGY

## Percentage: 15% of a Number

**Strategy**

Find 15% of 550.

$550 \div 10 = 55$     Step 1: Divide the number by 10.

$55 \div 2 = 27.5$     Step 2: Divide the quotient by 2.

$55 + 27.5 = 82.5$     Step 3: Add the quotients obtained in Steps 1 and 2.

15% of 550 = **82.5**

**Find each percentage mentally.**

1. 15% of 620 =

2. 15% of 350 =

3. 15% of 860 =

4. 15% of 920 =

5. 15% of 730 =

6. 15% of 190 =

7. 15% of 270 =

8. 15% of 400 =

9. 15% of 520 =

10. 15% of 780 =

STRATEGY

## Percentage: 20% of a Number

**Strategy**

Find 20% of 630.

630 ÷ 5 = 126

20% of 630 = **126**

❑ Divide the number by 5 to find the answer.

**Find each percentage mentally.**

1.   20% of 150 =

2.   20% of 830 =

3.   20% of 945 =

4.   20% of 425 =

5.   20% of 535 =

6.   20% of 655 =

7.   20% of 386 =

8.   20% of 763 =

9.   20% of 295 =

10.   20% of 1,050 =

## GENERAL REVIEW 7

**Solve each problem mentally.**

1. Convert $\frac{1}{4}$ to a percentage.

2. 5% of 830 =

3. 15% of 680 =

4. 20% of 590 =

5. Convert $\frac{18}{25}$ to a percentage.

6. 20% of 1,960 =

7. 5% of 3,750 =

8. 20% of 4,655 =

9. Convert $\frac{2}{5}$ to a percentage.

10. 15% of 950 =

42

STRATEGY

## Percentage: 45% of a Number

**Strategy**

Find 45% of 300.

$300 \div 20 = 15$

$15 \times 9 = 135$

45% of 300 = **135**

❏ Divide the number by 20.

❏ Multiply the quotient by 9 to find the answer.

**Find each percentage mentally.**

**1.** 45% of 140 =

**2.** 45% of 620 =

**3.** 45% of 660 =

**4.** 45% of 1,220 =

**5.** 45% of 560 =

**6.** 45% of 480 =

**7.** 45% of 940 =

**8.** 45% of 360 =

**9.** 45% of 2,460 =

**10.** 45% of 3,780 =

STRATEGY

## Squaring Numbers Ending with 5

**Strategy**

Find the value of $15^2$.

Step 1: To find the first few digits of the answer,

$1 \times (1 + 1) = 1 \times 2$
$= \mathbf{2}$

❑ Multiply the tens digit of the number by the number one more than itself.

Step 2: To find the last two digits of the answer,

$5 \times 5 = \mathbf{25}$

❑ Multiply the ones digit of the number by itself.

$15^2 = \mathbf{225}$

Note: To find the first few digits of a three-digit number ending with 5, multiply the first two digits of the number by the number one more than itself.

**Solve each problem mentally.**

1. $25^2 =$

2. $35^2 =$

3. $45^2 =$

4. $55^2 =$

5. $65^2 =$

6. $75^2 =$

7. $85^2 =$

8. $95^2 =$

9. $105^2 =$

10. $115^2 =$

# 38 STRATEGY

## Squaring Numbers Beginning with 9

**Strategy**

Find the value of $91^2$.

Step 1: To find the first few digits of the answer,

$100 - 91 = 9$

$100 - 9 - 9 = \textbf{82}$

❏ Subtract the number from 100. Subtract the difference from 100 twice.

Step 2: To find the last two digits of the answer,

$9 \times 9 = \textbf{81}$

❏ Multiply the difference obtained in Step 1 by itself.

$91^2 = \textbf{8,281}$

Note: When calculating the last two digits, write a 0 in the tens place if the product is a single digit.

**Solve each problem mentally.**

1. $92^2 =$

2. $95^2 =$

3. $99^2 =$

4. $97^2 =$

5. $90^2 =$

6. $93^2 =$

7. $96^2 =$

8. $98^2 =$

9. $94^2 =$

10. $91^2 =$

## Squaring Numbers Ending with 7

**Strategy**

Find the value of $87^2$.

Step 1: To find the last digit of the answer,

$7 \times 7 = 4\textcircled{9}$ ❑ Multiply the ones digit by itself.

Step 2: To find the next-to-last digit of the answer,

$(8 + 1) \times 4$
$= 9 \times 4$
$= 3\textcircled{6}$

❑ Add 1 to the tens digit of the number. Multiply the sum by 4. Then, carry the tens digit of the product to the next step.

Step 3: To find the first few digits of the answer,

$8 \times (8 + 1) + 3$
$= (8 \times 9) + 3$
$= 72 + 3$
$= \textbf{75}$

❑ Multiply the tens digit by the number one more than itself. Add the digit carried from Step 2.

$87^2 = \textbf{7,569}$

**Solve each problem mentally.**

**I.** $57^2 =$

**2.** $97^2 =$

**3.** $47^2 =$

**4.** $17^2 =$

**5.** $77^2 =$

**6.** $37^2 =$

**7.** $67^2 =$

**8.** $117^2 =$

**9.** $27^2 =$

**10.** $107^2 =$

# GENERAL REVIEW 8

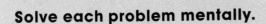

**Solve each problem mentally.**

1. 45% of 820 =

2. $135^2 =$

3. $93^2 =$

4. $127^2 =$

5. 45% of 420 =

6. $175^2 =$

7. $207^2 =$

8. $167^2 =$

9. $155^2 =$

10. $197^2 =$

# STRATEGY

## Squaring Numbers Ending with 8

**Strategy**

Find the value of $98^2$.

Step 1: To find the last digit of the answer,

$8 \times 8 = 6\textbf{④}$      ❏ Multiply the ones digit by itself.

Step 2: To find the next-to-last digit of the answer,

$(9 + 1) \times 6$
$= 10 \times 6$
$= 6\textbf{⓪}$

❏ Add 1 to the tens digit of the number. Multiply the sum by 6. Then, carry the tens digit of the product to the next step.

Step 3: To find the first few digits of the answer,

$9 \times (9 + 1) + 6$
$= (9 \times 10) + 6$
$= 90 + 6$
$= \textbf{96}$

❏ Multiply the tens digit by the number one more than itself. Add the digit carried from Step 2.

$98^2 = \textbf{9,604}$

**Solve each problem mentally.**

1. $28^2 =$

2. $48^2 =$

3. $68^2 =$

4. $58^2 =$

5. $88^2 =$

6. $18^2 =$

7. $78^2 =$

8. $38^2 =$

9. $108^2 =$

10. $118^2 =$

# 42

## STRATEGY

## Squaring Numbers Ending with 9

**Strategy**

Find the value of $29^2$.

Step 1: To find the last digit of the answer,

$9 \times 9 = 8①$  ❑ Multiply the ones digit by itself.

Step 2: To find the next-to-last digit of the answer,

$(2 + 1) \times 8$  ❑ Add 1 to the tens digit of the number. Multiply
$= 3 \times 8$  the sum by 8. Then, carry the tens digit of the
$= 2④$  product to the next step.

Step 3: To find the first few digits of the answer,

$2 \times (2 + 1) + 2$  ❑ Multiply the tens digit by the number one
$= (2 \times 3) + 2$  more than itself. Add the digit carried from
$= 6 + 2$  Step 2.
$= \mathbf{8}$

$29^2 = \mathbf{841}$

**Solve each problem mentally.**

1. $89^2 =$ 

2. $59^2 =$ 

3. $49^2 =$ 

4. $39^2 =$ 

5. $109^2 =$ 

6. $19^2 =$ 

7. $99^2 =$ 

8. $79^2 =$ 

9. $119^2 =$ 

10. $69^2 =$

## STRATEGY

# Squaring Numbers from 40 to 50

**Strategy**

Find the value of $44^2$.

Step 1: To find the last two digits of the answer,

$50 - 44 = 6$

$6 \times 6 = \textbf{36}$

❑ Subtract the number from 50. Multiply the difference by itself.

Step 2: To find the first two digits of the answer,

$25 - 6 = \textbf{19}$

❑ Subtract the difference obtained in Step 1 from 25.

$44^2 = \textbf{1,936}$

Note: If the calculation in Step 1 results in a one-digit number, write a 0 in the tens place.

## Solve each problem mentally.

1. $49^2 =$

2. $46^2 =$

3. $48^2 =$

4. $45^2 =$

5. $41^2 =$

6. $43^2 =$

7. $42^2 =$

8. $50^2 =$

9. $47^2 =$

10. $40^2 =$

STRATEGY

## Adding a Series of Consecutive Numbers

**Strategy**

Find the value of $1 + 2 + 3 + 4 + ... + 10$.

$10 \times (10 + 1)$
$= 10 \times 11$
$= 110$

$110 \div 2 = 55$

❑ Multiply the last number in the series by the number one more than itself.

❑ Divide the product by 2 to find the answer.

$1 + 2 + 3 + 4 + 5 + 6 + 7 + 8 + 9 + 10 =$ **55**

Note: This strategy only works if the series starts with 1.

**Solve each problem mentally.**

1. $1 + 2 + 3 + 4 + ... + 15 =$

2. $1 + 2 + 3 + 4 + ... + 20 =$

3. $1 + 2 + 3 + 4 + ... + 12 =$

4. $1 + 2 + 3 + 4 + ... + 40 =$

5. $1 + 2 + 3 + 4 + ... + 50 =$

6. $1 + 2 + 3 + 4 + ... + 25 =$

7. $1 + 2 + 3 + 4 + ... + 30 =$

8. $1 + 2 + 3 + 4 + ... + 18 =$

9. $1 + 2 + 3 + 4 + ... + 21 =$

10. $1 + 2 + 3 + 4 + ... + 29 =$

# WEEK 45

## STRATEGY

### Adding a Series of Numbers

**Strategy**

Find the value of 1 + 2 + 3 + 4 + 5 + 4 + 3 + 2 + 1.

$5^2 = 25$

1 + 2 + 3 + 4 + 5 + 4 + 3 + 2 + 1 = **25**

❑ Square the largest number in the series to find the answer.

Note: This strategy only works if the series starts with 1.

**Solve each problem mentally.**

1.  1 + 2 + 3 + 2 + 1 =

2.  1 + 2 + 3 + 4 + 5 + 6 + 5 + 4 + 3 + 2 + 1 =

3.  1 + 2 + 3 + 4 + 5 + 6 + 7 + 8 + 9 + 8 + 7 + 6 + 5 + 4 + 3 + 2 + 1 =

4.  1 + 2 + 3 + 4 + 3 + 2 + 1 =

5.  1 + 2 + 3 + 4 + 5 + 6 + 7 + 8 + 9 + 10 + 9 + 8 + 7 + 6 + 5 + 4 + 3 + 2 + 1 =

6.  1 + 2 + 3 + 4 + 5 + 6 + 7 + 8 + 9 + 10 + 11 + 12 + 11 + 10 + 9 + 8 + 7 + 6 + 5 + 4 + 3 + 2 + 1 =

7.  1 + 2 + 3 + 4 + 5 + 6 + 7 + 6 + 5 + 4 + 3 + 2 + 1 =

8.  1 + 2 + 3 + 4 + 5 + 6 + 7 + 8 + 7 + 6 + 5 + 4 + 3 + 2 + 1 =

9.  1 + 2 + 3 + 4 + 5 + 6 + 7 + 8 + 9 + 10 + 11 + 10 + 9 + 8 + 7 + 6 + 5 + 4 + 3 + 2 + 1 =

10. 1 + 2 + 3 + 4 + 5 + 6 + 7 + 8 + 9 + 10 + 11 + 12 + 13 + 14 + 15 + 14 + 13 + 12 + 11 + 10 + 9 + 8 + 7 + 6 + 5 + 4 + 3 + 2 + 1 =

# GENERAL REVIEW 9

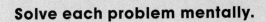

**Solve each problem mentally.**

1. $148^2 =$

2. $169^2 =$

3. $48^2 =$

4. $1 + 2 + 3 + 4 + ... + 29 =$

5. $1 + 2 + 3 + 4 + ... + 39 =$

6. $1 + 2 + 3 + 4 + 5 + 6 + 7 + 8 + 9 + 10 + 11 + 12 + 13 + 12 + 11 + 10 + 9 + 8 + 7 + 6 + 5 + 4 + 3 + 2 + 1 =$

7. $139^2 =$

8. $198^2 =$

9. $1 + 2 + 3 + 4 + ... + 99 =$

10. $1 + 2 + 3 + 4 + 5 + 6 + 7 + 8 + 9 + 10 + 11 + 12 + 13 + 14 + 15 + 16 + 17 + 18 + 19 + 20 + 19 + 18 + 17 + 16 + 15 + 14 + 13 + 12 + 11 + 10 + 9 + 8 + 7 + 6 + 5 + 4 + 3 + 2 + 1 =$

# GENERAL REVIEW 10

**Solve each problem mentally.**

1.  9,999,900 + 9,999,700 =

2.  49,999 – 9,980 =

3.  3,514 × 11 =

4.  4 × 15 × 25 =

5.  99 × 25 =

6.  10,225 ÷ 25 =

7.  81 × 50 =

8.  18 × 15 =

9.  2,816 ÷ 32 =

10. 632 – 236 =

# GENERAL REVIEW 11

**Solve each problem mentally.**

1. $\dfrac{1}{12} + \dfrac{4}{8} =$

2. $\dfrac{49}{84} \div 7 =$

3. Convert $\dfrac{17}{25}$ to a percentage.

4. $125^2 =$

5. $63 \times 12 =$

6. $1 + 2 + 3 + 4 + \ldots + 35 =$

7. Find the remainder of $7{,}838 \div 5$.

   R =

8. $3\dfrac{1}{5} \times 7\dfrac{1}{5} =$

9. $5\%$ of $780 =$

10. $\dfrac{9}{10} - \dfrac{1}{3} =$

# GENERAL REVIEW 12

**Solve each problem mentally.**

**1.** 923 − 329 =

**2.** 42 × 25 =

**3.** $8\frac{2}{3} \times 12 =$

**4.** 45% of 960 =

**5.** 1 + 2 + 3 + 4 + 5 + 6 + 7 + 6 + 5 + 4 + 3 + 2 + 1 =

**6.** Find the remainder of 7,358 ÷ 9.

**7.** 100,380 + 795,620 =

**8.** $147^2 =$

**9.** Convert $\frac{1}{5}$ to a percentage.

**10.** 125 × 206 × 8 =

R =

## GENERAL REVIEW 13

**Solve each problem mentally.**

1.  20% of 8,900 =

2.  Find the remainder of 3,015 ÷ 8.

3.  31 × 25 =

4.  123,450 + 810,050 =

5.  6,159 × 11 =

6.  5 × 58 × 20 =

7.  9,405 ÷ 45 =

8.  $7\frac{1}{3} \times 7\frac{2}{3}$ =

9.  $\frac{4}{7} + \frac{3}{8}$ =

10. 1 + 2 + 3 + 4 + ... + 40 =

R =

GENERAL REVIEW 14

**Solve each problem mentally.**

1. $12\frac{1}{3} \times 12\frac{2}{3} =$

2. Convert $\frac{22}{50}$ to a percentage.

3. 45% of 7,560 =

4. $187^2 =$

5. 1 + 2 + 3 + 4 + 5 + 6 + 7 + 8 + 9 + 10 + 11 + 12 + 13 + 14 + 15 + 16 + 17 + 18 + 17 + 16 + 15 + 14 + 13 + 12 + 11 + 10 + 9 + 8 + 7 + 6 + 5 + 4 + 3 + 2 + 1 =

6. 56 × 15 =

7. 9,999,960 + 9,999,988 =

8. Find the remainder of 8,726 ÷ 9.

9. $\frac{1}{9} + \frac{6}{11} =$

10. $49^2 =$

R =

58

# GENERAL REVIEW 15

**Solve each problem mentally.**

1. $5 \times 43 \times 20 =$

2. $399,970 - 190,950 =$

3. $1 + 2 + 3 + 4 + ... + 300 =$

4. $199^2 =$

5. $20\dfrac{1}{2} \times 20\dfrac{1}{2} =$

6. $7,808 \div 64 =$

7. $1,771 \times 11 =$

8. $\dfrac{27}{42} \div 3 =$

9. $5\% \text{ of } 790 =$

10. Find the remainder of $8,029 \div 8$.

R =

# Notes

# ANSWER KEY *Mental Math Level 5*

### WEEK 1
1. 1,999,991
2. 19,999,890
3. 1,998,000
4. 1,999,590
5. 1,999,799
6. 19,999,887
7. 19,999,620
8. 19,999,498
9. 1,999,698
10. 19,999,886

### WEEK 2
1. 78,000
2. 453,290
3. 1,051,000
4. 1,181,100
5. 600,000
6. 1,147,000
7. 1,200,000
8. 998,620
9. 876,000
10. 795,000

### WEEK 3
1. 600,004
2. 300,100
3. 300,099
4. 200,050
5. 100,199
6. 300,060
7. 400,100
8. 10,110
9. 10,102
10. 310,093

### WEEK 4
1. 693
2. 594
3. 396
4. 99
5. 792
6. 495
7. 99
8. 198
9. 594
10. 495

### WEEK 5
1. 19,999,875
2. 198
3. 589,000
4. 19,999,884
5. 400,911
6. 300,008
7. 99
8. 1,999,880
9. 792
10. 104,500

### WEEK 6
1. 3,900
2. 7,700
3. 5,500
4. 9,600
5. 4,800
6. 6,400
7. 2,600
8. 1,900
9. 5,200
10. 3,300

### WEEK 7
1. 213,000
2. 743,000
3. 316,000
4. 976,000
5. 628,000
6. 816,000
7. 511,000
8. 177,000
9. 401,000
10. 837,000

### WEEK 8
1. 2,200
2. 1,850
3. 950
4. 1,400
5. 3,300
6. 4,650
7. 4,200
8. 3,550
9. 2,650
10. 4,950

### WEEK 9
1. 13,574
2. 33,341
3. 49,742
4. 49,753
5. 69,564
6. 27,797
7. 58,476
8. 39,974
9. 77,297
10. 37,983

### WEEK 10
1. 4,300
2. 4,400
3. 716,000
4. 67,452
5. 8,100
6. 15,587
7. 1,800
8. 2,800
9. 26,664
10. 35,000

### WEEK 11
1. 456
2. 828
3. 516
4. 648
5. 984
6. 900
7. 1,092
8. 216
9. 576
10. 348

### WEEK 12
1. 675
2. 435
3. 1,005
4. 1,380
5. 510
6. 255
7. 1,290
8. 315
9. 1,350
10. 1,095

### WEEK 13
1. 775
2. 550
3. 1,100
4. 2,325
5. 925
6. 300
7. 1,575
8. 1,300
9. 2,175
10. 1,850

### WEEK 14
1. 1,800
2. 850
3. 2,400
4. 3,150
5. 4,700
6. 1,450
7. 2,750
8. 3,900
9. 4,050
10. 3,450

### WEEK 15
1. 480
2. 1,155
3. 950
4. 672
5. 2,650
6. 1,068
7. 465
8. 1,800
9. 270
10. 3,050

### WEEK 16
1. 90
2. 96
3. 111
4. 95
5. 106
6. 217
7. 84
8. 121
9. 87
10. 182

## WEEK 17
1. 4
2. 3
3. 3
4. 2
5. 4
6. 2
7. 1
8. 1
9. 3
10. 1

## WEEK 18
1. 7
2. 3
3. 1
4. 7
5. 1
6. 2
7. 4
8. 6
9. 1
10. 6

## WEEK 19
1. 2
2. 8
3. 2
4. 4
5. 8
6. 1
7. 8
8. 6
9. 2
10. 3

## WEEK 20
1. 92
2. 2
3. 7
4. 8
5. 65
6. 88
7. 3
8. 73
9. 1
10. 4

## WEEK 21
1. 48
2. 363
3. 86
4. 336
5. 209
6. 250
7. 314
8. 163
9. 149
10. 342

## WEEK 22
1. $\frac{28}{32}$
2. $\frac{59}{60}$
3. $\frac{7}{6}$
4. $\frac{19}{28}$
5. $\frac{25}{42}$
6. $\frac{47}{36}$
7. $\frac{114}{132}$
8. $\frac{124}{90}$
9. $\frac{46}{48}$
10. $\frac{89}{63}$

## WEEK 23
1. $\frac{1}{35}$
2. $\frac{26}{48}$
3. $\frac{2}{15}$
4. $\frac{9}{36}$
5. $\frac{17}{63}$
6. $\frac{3}{10}$
7. $\frac{4}{60}$
8. $\frac{52}{132}$
9. $\frac{41}{90}$
10. $\frac{5}{12}$

## WEEK 24
1. 57
2. 69
3. 26
4. 43
5. 78
6. 58
7. 111
8. 202
9. 34
10. 54

## WEEK 25
1. $\frac{17}{30}$
2. $\frac{15}{72}$
3. $\frac{7}{22}$
4. 306
5. 325
6. $\frac{56}{99}$
7. 204
8. 137
9. 399
10. 363

## WEEK 26
1. $2\frac{1}{4}$
2. $20\frac{1}{4}$
3. $42\frac{1}{4}$
4. $30\frac{1}{4}$
5. $12\frac{1}{4}$
6. $72\frac{1}{4}$
7. $110\frac{1}{4}$
8. $156\frac{1}{4}$
9. $90\frac{1}{4}$
10. $56\frac{1}{4}$

## WEEK 27

1. $17\frac{1}{16}$
2. $31\frac{1}{9}$
3. $206\frac{1}{25}$
4. $35\frac{1}{16}$
5. $22\frac{1}{100}$
6. $131\frac{1}{4}$
7. $55\frac{1}{4}$
8. $35\frac{1}{49}$
9. $19\frac{1}{81}$
10. $100\frac{1}{25}$

## WEEK 28

1. $110\frac{2}{9}$
2. $20\frac{6}{25}$
3. $56\frac{12}{49}$
4. $12\frac{8}{81}$
5. $30\frac{2}{9}$
6. $72\frac{8}{36}$
7. $90\frac{21}{100}$
8. $42\frac{5}{36}$
9. $132\frac{12}{64}$
10. $6\frac{35}{144}$

## WEEK 29

1. $\frac{1}{12}$
2. $\frac{3}{50}$
3. $\frac{4}{15}$
4. $\frac{1}{12}$
5. $\frac{3}{25}$
6. $\frac{3}{20}$
7. $\frac{1}{5}$
8. $\frac{3}{50}$
9. $\frac{5}{12}$
10. $\frac{5}{22}$

## WEEK 30

1. $132\frac{1}{4}$
2. $34\frac{1}{36}$
3. $132\frac{6}{25}$
4. $\frac{3}{20}$
5. $122\frac{1}{121}$
6. $240\frac{1}{4}$
7. $90\frac{12}{49}$
8. $\frac{1}{16}$
9. $67\frac{1}{81}$
10. $\frac{1}{12}$

## WEEK 31

1. 45%
2. 26%
3. 50%
4. 52%
5. 80%
6. 58%
7. 60%
8. 75%
9. 60%
10. 50%

## WEEK 32

1. 7
2. 11
3. 17.5
4. 23
5. 27.5
6. 48
7. 35.5
8. 30.9
9. 61.5
10. 123.1

## WEEK 33

1. 93
2. 52.5
3. 129
4. 138
5. 109.5
6. 28.5
7. 40.5
8. 60
9. 78
10. 117

## WEEK 34

1. 30
2. 166
3. 189
4. 85
5. 107
6. 131
7. 77.2
8. 152.6
9. 59
10. 210

## WEEK 35

1. 25%
2. 41.5
3. 102
4. 118
5. 72%
6. 392
7. 187.5
8. 931
9. 40%
10. 142.5

## WEEK 36

1. 63
2. 279
3. 297
4. 549
5. 252
6. 216
7. 423
8. 162
9. 1,107
10. 1,701

## WEEK 37

1. 625
2. 1,225
3. 2,025
4. 3,025
5. 4,225
6. 5,625
7. 7,225
8. 9,025
9. 11,025
10. 13,225

## WEEK 38

1. 8,464
2. 9,025
3. 9,801
4. 9,409
5. 8,100
6. 8,649
7. 9,216
8. 9,604
9. 8,836
10. 8,281

## WEEK 39

1. 3,249
2. 9,409
3. 2,209
4. 289
5. 5,929
6. 1,369
7. 4,489
8. 13,689
9. 729
10. 11,449

## WEEK 40

1. 369
2. 18,225
3. 8,649
4. 16,129
5. 189
6. 30,625
7. 42,849
8. 27,889
9. 24,025
10. 38,809

## WEEK 41

1. 784
2. 2,304
3. 4,624
4. 3,364
5. 7,744
6. 324
7. 6,084
8. 1,444
9. 11,664
10. 13,924

## WEEK 42

1. 7,921
2. 3,481
3. 2,401
4. 1,521
5. 11,881
6. 361
7. 9,801
8. 6,241
9. 14,161
10. 4,761

## WEEK 43

1. 2,401
2. 2,116
3. 2,304
4. 2,025
5. 1,681
6. 1,849
7. 1,764
8. 2,500
9. 2,209
10. 1,600

## WEEK 44

1. 120
2. 210
3. 78
4. 820
5. 1,275
6. 325
7. 465
8. 171
9. 231
10. 435

## WEEK 45

1. 9
2. 36
3. 81
4. 16
5. 100
6. 144
7. 49
8. 64
9. 121
10. 225

## WEEK 46

1. 21,904
2. 28,561
3. 2,304
4. 435
5. 780
6. 169
7. 19,321
8. 39,204
9. 4,950
10. 400

## WEEK 47

1. 19,999,600
2. 40,019
3. 38,654
4. 1,500
5. 2,475
6. 409
7. 4,050
8. 270
9. 88
10. 396

## WEEK 48

1. $\frac{56}{96}$
2. $\frac{1}{12}$
3. 68%
4. 15,625
5. 756
6. 630
7. 3
8. $23\frac{1}{25}$
9. 39
10. $\frac{17}{30}$

## WEEK 49

1. 594
2. 1,050
3. 104
4. 432
5. 49
6. 5
7. 896,000
8. 21,609
9. 20%
10. 206,000

## WEEK 50

1. 1,780
2. 7
3. 775
4. 933,500
5. 67,749
6. 5,800
7. 209
8. $56\frac{2}{9}$
9. $\frac{53}{56}$
10. 820

## WEEK 51

1. $156\frac{2}{9}$
2. 44%
3. 3,402
4. 34,969
5. 324
6. 840
7. 19,999,948
8. 5
9. $\frac{65}{99}$
10. 2,401

## WEEK 52

1. 4,300
2. 209,020
3. 45,150
4. 39,601
5. $420\frac{1}{4}$
6. 122
7. 19,481
8. $\frac{3}{14}$
9. 39.5
10. 5

64

© Singapore Asian Publications (S) Pte Ltd